MONSTER ⚙ MACHINES

SUPER BIKES

DAVID JEFFERIS

Belitha Press

First published in the UK in 2001 by
Belitha Press Limited,
an imprint of Chrysalis Books plc,
64 Brewery Road, London N7 9NT

Paperback edition first published
in 2002

Copyright © David Jefferis/Alpha
Communications 2001

Educational advisor
Julie Stapleton
Design and editorial production
Alpha Communications
Additional picture research
Kay Rowley

Diagrams by
Gavin Page/Design Shop

ISBN 1 84138 191 8 (hardback)
ISBN 1 84138 387 2 (paperback)

Printed in Hong Kong.

10 9 8 7 6 5 4 3 2 1 (hardback)
10 9 8 7 6 5 4 3 2 1 (paperback)

British Library Cataloguing in
Publication Data for this book is
available from the British Library.

Acknowledgements
*We wish to thank the following
individuals and organizations for
their help and assistance and for
supplying material in their
collections:*
All-Sport Photographic Ltd,
Alpha Archive, Tim Andrew,
Roland Brown, Paul Bryant,
CCM Motorcycles, Michael Cooper,
Dan Harris, Honda Motor Co,
Phil Masters, Andrew Morland,
Don Morley, Quadrant Picture
Library, Suzuki Motor Co

▲ A super bike rider takes
the lead in a race. The fat
rear tyre gives a good grip
on the track when speeding
up and when cornering.

CONTENTS

⚙ **TECH-TALK**

Look for the cog and blue box for explanations of technical terms.

👁 **EYE-VIEW**

Look for the eye and yellow box for eyewitness accounts.

ON TWO WHEELS

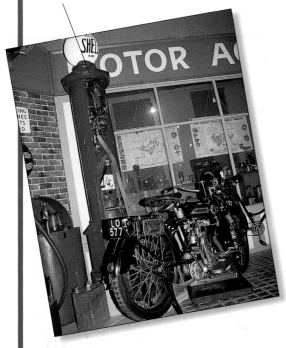

fuel pump

▲ A super bike of the 1920s waits to be refuelled.

A super bike is a great-looking motorcycle that goes fast, and takes corners easily.

A super bike has a powerful engine for speed. But taking bends safely is just as important as speed on straight roads. So the best super bikes have easy handling for taking corners well.

Crowded roads mean that slowing down safely is important. A super bike must have powerful brakes, so the rider can come to a halt quickly and smoothly.

Styling counts as well. The best super bikes have to look good!

◄ Motorcycle racing is a popular sport. Here riders battle for position in an off-road race called moto-cross.

front brake lever

plastic fairing

side stand

disc brake

▲ The Suzuki 600 is designed to look like a racing machine. The plastic bodywork, or fairing, keeps the wind off the rider's chest at speed, giving a smoother ride.

⚙ COMING TO A HALT SAFELY

Almost all motorcycles have disc brakes for good stopping power. The idea is very simple – pulling on the brake lever makes a pair of brake pads grip a steel disc tightly, like fingers squeezing a coin (*see page 31*). The disc is joined to the wheel, so wheel and bike slow down as the pads grip tighter.

SUPER BIKE POWER

fuel tank   *engine*

frame

▲ This early bike had its engine over the front wheel. The fuel tank lay below the saddle.

The heart of any super bike is the engine. It is normally carried by the metal frame, and usually drives the back wheel with a chain.

Designers of early motorcycles could not make up their minds where to put the engine. They tried all sorts of places. One bike even towed its engine on a trailer!

Then, in 1909, the Werner motorcycle was built. This bike had its engine placed at the bottom of the frame. And this is the way motorcycles have been built, ever since.

▶ Engines may be small or large, but nowadays they are always in roughly the same place. This is in the metal frame, low down for good balance.

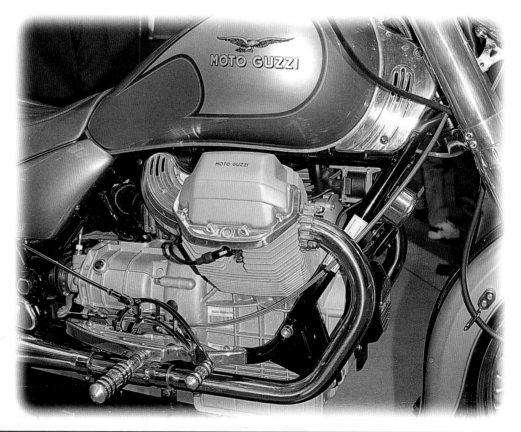

⚙ FASTER AND FASTER

The first motorcycles could go no faster than 20 km/h, but soon more powerful engines allowed higher speeds. In 1907, US rider Glenn Curtiss raced along a Florida beach at 220 km/h. He rode so fast that many people thought he had cheated, and his record was never recognized.

▲ Racing machines have the most powerful engines of all, and many can travel at speeds of 200 km/h or more. Super bike racing is an international sport – here an Italian rides a Japanese bike on a US track.

▶ Even the most carefully prepared super bike sometimes needs a push-start!

SAFE RIDING

Cars and trucks have bumpers, seat belts and other safety features for protection. Super bikes have none of these, so riding with great care is essential.

▲ Safety gear is most important, starting with a good helmet.

leather gloves protect hands

The safest riders are those who learn 'defensive riding'. Using this, you check all the time for danger – perhaps a slippery patch of ice, or spilled oil.

You look out for other people, and vehicles, in case someone pulls out suddenly. In this way defensive riders try to avoid an accident before it happens.

jacket has extra-strong plastic elbow guards

LEARNING TO RIDE WELL

1 Riders should check bikes are in safe working order before moving off. Practise on quiet trails before riding on roads.

2 Controls should all work properly.

3 Check around before moving off.

👁 TEACHING BEGINNERS TO RIDE

'Training is essential for bikers on busy roads. Learners bring their own bikes or use ours. Slow riding is difficult, as bikes get wobbly as they slow down. We have a pattern of traffic cones for riders to thread through – the rider who goes slowest without putting a foot down wins a prize!' *Bike trainer*

▲ On a racing track, riders are experts and the traffic is going the same way. Public roads are full of vehicles going in different directions. Car drivers often do not see bikes, so riders need to take extra care.

4 Practise smooth starts on hills.

5 Slow riding can be difficult to perfect.

6 Practise riding on rough ground.

7 Finish off with a speedy burn-up!

EASY RIDERS

▲ This Harley-Davidson of 1912 used a leather belt to drive the wheel, instead of a chain.

Not everyone likes riding fast. Many bikers like to sit back and cruise along. They are called easy riders.

To many bikers, easy-rider bikes are not very exciting – a bit like sitting in a two-wheel armchair. But easy riders say that comfort and style are more important than speed.

The most popular easy-rider machine is a US classic, the Harley-Davidson. Harleys are famous for their great looks. Top models include a hi-fi stereo and squashy seats. There is even a helmet intercom, so driver and passenger can talk to each other easily.

▼ The owner of this Harley FLH has added many extras, including chrome wheels and a hand-made seat.

▲ Customizing a bike is changing its looks to make it individual, for instance by spraying on your own paint style. Harleys are tops with customizers.

▶ This custom bike has a special paint job, and a much more powerful engine than usual.

👁 **EASY RIDING ON A 'HOG'**

'Big Harleys are nicknamed Hogs, mainly because they are so big. I like to go on vacation on my Electra Glide. On open stretches of highway, I can set the cruise control to keep my hog at a set speed. I then sit back and enjoy the country rolling past. What a great ride! ' *Harley rider*

EMERGENCY PATROL

Super bikes are essential tools for the emergency services. They are used by medical and police units, and as roadside help for people whose cars have broken down.

blue flashing lights warn other road users

▶ A paramedic bike is fast, though there is room to carry only a basic set of medical equipment.

medical kit carried in storage boxes

High-speed medical help can be a life-saver for anyone who falls ill suddenly or is in an accident. A super bike's size is a big advantage on the roads. A trained rider can weave through traffic-choked streets and bring help much quicker than an ambulance crew can.

reflective patterns glow brightly at night, so the bike shows up on the road

◎ THANKS FOR YOUR HELP, BIKERS!

'I was knocked over by a truck in rush hour. The smash caused a massive traffic jam, but it was only a few minutes before the paramedic arrived on his bike. It was in the nick of time, as I was losing blood fast, but he took care of me' *Accident victim*

▶ Many police forces use helicopters as 'eyes in the sky' for bike and car patrols down on the ground.

⚙ CATCHING CRIMINALS

Crime-fighting police use bikes, cars and air patrols together. At night, helicopters can light up the ground with powerful searchlights. The heli-police can guide bike or car patrols to the scene by radio. The crime-fighting advantage of a motorbike is that a police rider can chase through busy traffic, or go up alleys that are too narrow for police cars to enter.

◀ A paramedic jots down details of the next job. He talks to base using radio gear on the bike.

RACING BIKES

Super bikes that are built for winning races are very different from standard machines made for riding on the highway.

▲ Extra-strong brakes are an essential part of all racing super bikes.

The engine is the core of a racing bike. Designers work hard to make the most powerful engine possible. The engine must be reliable, too. A fast bike is no good if the engine fails half-way through a race.

Race tyres have no tread pattern. In dry weather, plain rubber gives the best grip – it is called a 'slick'. Wet weather tyres have a deep centre channel to drain away water.

👁 KNEE-DOWN IN THE CORNERS

'The first time I saw top riders taking bends at speed, I thought they were going to take their legs off. Bikes lean over so far that the riders' knees graze the track, at over 130 km/h! Tough knee-pads are essential gear for all riders.'
Race enthusiast

▶ A smooth riding style helps the fat rear tyre grip in corners.

◀ Ouch! Crashes are common in racing, though serious injuries are rare. Tough leather protection is still best, though fire crews are always ready to help at a moment's notice.

▲ Riders crouch behind the screen. This cuts down wind blast, helping the bike go faster.

OFF-ROAD RIDING

Special bikes are needed for riding off the road. They must be built to cope with bumps, ruts, mud and dust.

Off-road bikes have several design features to deal with rough country. The engine and frame are set high, to avoid rocks or tree roots that might be in the way. The bikes have massive springs, to give the rider a smooth ride over bumps. Tyres are specially designed for good grip on slippery or muddy surfaces.

▼ Off-road riders can cross country by following marked trails.

mudguard set high

spring for back wheel

⚙ GETTING A GRIP

Off-road bikes use tyres that have a deep-cut, chunky pattern or tread. This type of tread allows a tyre to sink into mud, yet grip enough to keep going. Tyres for road bikes have a smoother surface. This is fine for highways, but almost useless in mud.

off-road tyres are called knobblies because of the way they look

◄ Off-road bikes have chunky tyres and good springs for riding safely through mud and dirt.

MOTO-CROSS

Moto-cross is an exciting off-road sport. In a race, bikes hurtle round twisty circuits, tyres spinning in the mud, as riders battle for the lead.

▲ Bike and rider fly through the air after hitting a bump.

Moto-cross, or MX for short, is great to watch. You can usually get close to the action. Sometimes you may feel too close – if you are covered in mud from spinning tyres!

Apart from the usual riding gear, MX riders wear plastic body armour. They need this in case they are thrown off at high speed – without protection, bones are easily broken.

▼ MX riders roar into the first corner of a race. It is narrow, and the first rider through takes the 'hole shot'.

⚙ ENDURO RACING

Enduros are long off-road races. Enduro bikes look like MX machines but riders compete on routes such as the 10 000 km Wynn's Safari, across Australia. Here riders cope with a route that ranges from wet swamp to dry desert. Enduro riders have to keep spot-on timing. They also do their own repairs if they have a puncture or break down.

◀ MX riders also race on specially-built, stadium tracks.

👁 RACING IN THE HEAT

'My first moto-cross race was held on a really hot day. My big problem during the event was sweat dripping into my eyes. For much of the race I had to keep blinking fast to keep my vision clear! By the finish I couldn't believe how tired I felt. Every muscle ached, and I was so weak that I nearly fell off the bike. But at least I didn't finish last!' *MX rider*

RECORD BREAKERS

When a rider plans to set a record, the bike has to be ready and in top condition. Items such as the timing equipment also need to be accurate.

◄ Good weather helps a record breaker. If the wind is too strong, the bike might be blown off course, or slowed down.

Record-breaking super bikes need careful preparation. The engine and exhaust system need adjusting to give the bike more power.

Special high-speed tyres are vital. These are made of stronger materials than usual, otherwise the rubber might spin off the metal wheel, ripping apart to cause a high-speed crash.

► Dan Harris powers away along an aircraft runway, trying for the UK two-wheel Land Speed Record, in 1999. His speed will be recorded over a 402m stretch in the middle. Dan had only 1.2 km in which to get up to speed, but still took the record at 343 km/h.

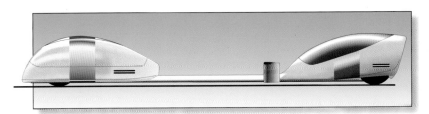

◄ This is a US design for a speed record-breaker. The engine is placed in the front pod, the rider sits inside the back section.

rider crouches low to avoid wind blast

⚙ CUTTING THROUGH THE AIR

Aerodynamics is the science of shaping machines to move easily through the air. Smooth, rounded shapes are usually best, but rider Dan Harris added some details for his record attempt. He used tape to seal the gaps between his gloves, boots and leather suit. He also used tape to seal his helmet visor shut.

WILD RIDES

The wide world of super bikes includes some unusual types of racing. Stunt riders have all sorts of tricks!

▲ Ice-racing bikes use tyres like the one shown here. For grip, it's studded with dozens of needle-sharp spikes, each 30 mm long.

Ice racing is popular in Scandinavia and East Europe. The tracks are usually circular, so fierce-looking spiked tyres are needed to grip the ice. Riders protect their knees and elbows by padding them with lengths of old tyre.

Speedway riders hurtle round an oval track. The track is covered with cinders. This loose surface lets a rider slide the back wheel around corners, balancing the bike with one foot sliding in the dirt.

Stunt riders train to give crowds thrills at shows. Many stunts are dangerous, and riders have to train hard to do these safely.

► Speedway riders roar around a 400m oval track, covered with cinders. Races are usually just four laps, so they are over very quickly.

◀ Constant training is needed to make a stunt work well. Stunt riders make stunts like this look easy. Even so, a small mistake can mean serious injury and a wrecked bike.

👁 THROUGH THE FLAMES

'My daredevil stunt team performs all year round. We train hard between shows to keep our skills top-notch. Timing of stunts is vital. For instance, riding through the flames has to be exactly right. If you are slow taking off the ramp, you could be badly burnt. I missed the ramp once, when a chunk of flaming hay blew on my helmet. I fell off the bike but managed to roll clear!' *Stunt rider*

roll hoop

FUTURE BIKES

Bike designers are working to make safer super bikes, and bikes to beat city traffic jams.

The German BMW company have built the odd-looking C1 bike to make riding safer. It has tiny wheels and looks top-heavy, but in a crash, the rider should escape unhurt. To ride away on a C1, you strap yourself to the seat, and have a strong 'roll hoop' over your head for protection.

Machines like this could help to make riding safer in the future for many bikers.

▲ As well as giving crash protection, the C1 keeps the rider dry. There is even a windscreen wiper.

◄ These pictures show a C1 crash test. The bike's seat belt and roll bars give the rider more protection than on a normal motorbike.

⚙ BEATING THE TRAFFIC

In many countries, cities are so choked with traffic that driving is difficult. Mini bikes called motor scooters are one answer to the problem. People can ride round the traffic, and parking them is easy. Helmets and wet-weather gear can be kept in storage bins under the seat.

storage room under seat

▼ Big-engine super bikes are sold on style as well as being good to ride. This is one idea for a near-future super bike.

the first motorcycle had a wooden frame

SUPER BIKE FACTS

Here are some facts and figures from the history of super bikes.

Flaming saddle

The first motorcycle was made in Germany by Gottlieb Daimler and Wilhelm Maybach. Daimler's son Paul rode it first, but had to leap off after a few minutes – the engine was so hot that it set the saddle on fire!

Gleaming chrome

Easy-rider bikes such as Harley-Davidsons look so good because they have shiny chromed parts. The first chromed bike was a 1929 British Rudge speedway machine. Before then, the usual finish was black paint over metal.

Danger race

The oldest race held on public roads is the Tourist Trophy, or TT. The course is a 61-km loop around the Isle of Man. The TT has been held every year since 1907, and thousands of bikers still go to watch. The course is closed to the public during races, but riders agree the narrow and winding course is the most dangerous in the world.

Rocket man

In 1928, German inventor Fritz von Opel built a new super bike. It had a normal engine, with six rockets fixed at the back. Opel tried breaking speed records but gave up the idea after the rockets nearly exploded!

▲ All easy-rider bikes have shiny chromed parts.

Baking bread

German rider Wilhelm Hertz roared along at 290 km/h in 1951, to take the world motorcycle speed record. To build up his muscles for the record attempt, Hertz took up breadmaking. He thought that kneading lots of dough toughened his arms and shoulders better than a workout. He also made very tasty bread!

Hot gripper

Rubber grips best when it is warm and sticky, but not so hot that it melts. During a race, a bike's rear tyre becomes hot enough to boil a kettle. The rubber can hit 125°C or more.

collectable tin lunch box shows Evel Knievel's rocket-bike flight

Snake River stunt

US ace Evel Knievel is still king of the stunt riders. In 1974 he planned to ride the *SkyCycle X2* rocket-bike 400 metres through the air across Snake River, Idaho, USA. The bike took off, but a parachute opened by mistake and slowed the bike down. Knievel landed on the other side with just a few metres to spare.

Super bikes at war

In World War 2, many bike ideas were tried out. These included a micro-machine to be parachuted from a plane into enemy country. Also in World War 2, the Germans built a bike with tank-tracks, for riding through mud and sand.

◄ Fast work is hot work for a set of racing tyres.

SUPER BIKE WORDS

Here are some technical terms used in this book.

aerodynamics
Science of shaping machines to slip easily through the air. Smooth, slim shapes are better than boxy shapes.

customize
Changing a normal bike, to make a one-off machine for a particular rider. Changes may be simple, like a special paint job, or may involve more work. This may include specially-shaped parts and improvements to the engine.

disc brake
Brake with two pads that grip either side of a metal disc.

drive chain
Metal chain that turns a bike's back wheel. It is a tougher version of a bicycle chain.

enduro
Long race in which riders keep to a timetable. Arrive late (or early) at a check point, and you lose marks.

exhaust system
Pipe that takes waste gases from the engine. It ends with a silencer unit. This reduces noise.

fairing
Sections covering a bike, to improve aerodynamics.

frame
Metal 'backbone' of a motorcycle. Bikes with strong and stiff frames are usually good-handling machines. A weak frame may bend, leading to wobbly steering.

▼ Aerodynamic fairing on an Agusta super bike, made in Italy.

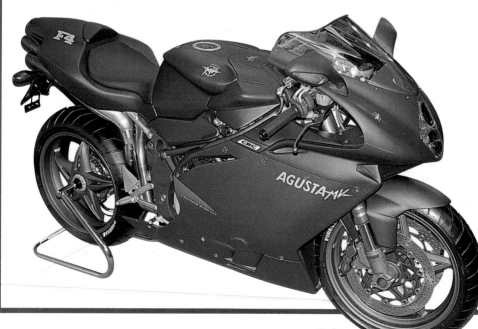

handlebar

Metal cross-tube used to steer a bike. Engine and brake controls are on the handgrips at each end.

handling

The way in which a motorcycle can be ridden. Good handling bikes can be flicked through corners easily and smoothly. Poor handling bikes need careful control.

Super bike engine

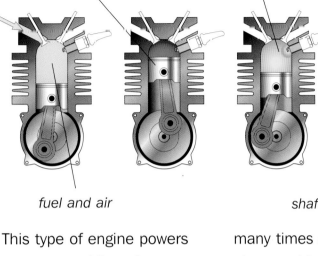
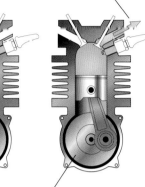

piston   *explosion*   *burnt gas exhaust*

fuel and air   *shaft turns round*

This type of engine powers many super bikes. It uses a piston inside a cylinder. A gassy mixture of fuel and air is burnt, and small explosions drive the piston up and down, many times a second. A piston rod joins a shaft, which turns round as the piston moves. The shaft goes to the gearbox, and a drive chain turns the rear wheel.

hole shot

The first bend on a moto-cross (MX) course. MX riders start in a wide line abreast. The hole-shot bend is purposely narrow, so riders scrabble to be first through and take an early lead.

intercom

Sound system that lets a bike rider and passenger talk to each other easily. Headphones and microphone are linked by cable.

moto-cross (MX)

Off-road dirt race. MX courses are mostly twisting circuits on rough ground. Bulldozers shift soil to make jumps, dips and gulleys. Temporary MX courses can also be made for stadium races.

super bike

There is no official meaning. It is really any big and fast motorcycle that looks good, handles well, and has a powerful engine.

twist-grip

Right handlebar control for the engine. Twisting the grip back increases engine speed.

tread

Pattern of grooves, cut in a tyre. They channel rainwater away so that the tyre does not slip on a wet day.

SUPER BIKE PROJECTS

These mini-projects show you some of the science in the world of super bikes

MUD-PLUGGER TYRES

On and off-road tyres work in different ways. The rough surface of a tarmac surface digs into the smooth rubber of a tyre – off-road tyres are designed to sink into the dirt and push against it.

tyre sinks into dirt

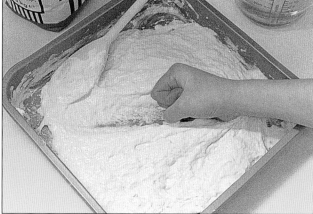

1 For this mud-plugger experiment, you need flour and water, plus a storage container. Mix up some flour and water until you get a thick paste, about the same thickness as off-road mud.

2 Now ball your fist and sink it into the paste. Move your fist to one side, and you should find that there is little resistance and your fist slides easily. This is the same as a road tyre slipping on a muddy surface.

SQUASHY PNEUMATICS

The earliest tyres were made of metal. Then came solid rubber, and finally the pneumatic tyres of today. These have a rubber casing, with air pumped inside to act as a squashy 'air spring'. This makes vehicles comfortable to ride in.

1 Blow up a balloon and tie the neck. Put the balloon on the floor and gently sit on it. Bounce up and down to feel the air spring in action.

2 To see what happens when a tyre has a puncture, poke the balloon with a sharp pencil. All the air cushioning is gone!

3 Wash your hand, and open out your fingers to make a claw. Dig into the flour paste and see the difference. Your fingers are like the knobbly pattern of an off-road tyre and provide quite good grip.

pinch coin firmly

DISC BRAKE POWER

To see how a disc brake works, pinch either side of a coin with your fingers. This is the same action as the pads of a disc brake. Squeeze hard and try to move the coin with your other hand. It should be almost impossible.

INDEX